LET'S READ AV² BY WEIGL
ADDED VALUE • AUDIO VISUAL

Go to **www.av2books.com**, and enter this book's unique code.

BOOK CODE

E953375

AV² by Weigl brings you media enhanced books that support active learning.

AV² provides enriched content that supplements and complements this book. Weigl's AV² books strive to create inspired learning and engage young minds in a total learning experience.

Your AV² Media Enhanced books come alive with...

 **Audio**
Listen to sections of the book read aloud.

 **Key Words**
Study vocabulary, and complete a matching word activity.

 **Video**
Watch informative video clips.

 **Quizzes**
Test your knowledge.

 **Embedded Weblinks**
Gain additional information for research.

 **Slide Show**
View images and captions, and prepare a presentation.

 **Try This!**
Complete activities and hands-on experiments.

... and much, much more!

Published by AV² by Weigl.
350 5th Avenue, 59th Floor New York, NY 10118
Websites: www.av2books.com www.weigl.com

Copyright ©2016 AV² by Weigl
All rights reserved. No part of this publication may be reproduced, stored in a retrieval system, or transmitted in any form or by any means, electronic, mechanical, photocopying, recording, or otherwise, without the prior written permission of the publisher.

Library of Congress Cataloging-in-Publication Data
Carr, Aaron.
  Woodpeckers / Aaron Carr.
    pages cm. -- (Animals in my backyard)
  Includes bibliographical references and index.
  ISBN 978-1-4896-2950-0 (hard cover : alk. paper) -- ISBN 978-1-4896-2951-7 (soft cover : alk. paper) -- ISBN 978-1-4896-2952-4 (single user ebook) -- ISBN 978-1-4896-2953-1 (multi-user ebook)
  1. Woodpeckers--Juvenile literature. I. Title.
  QL696.P56C37 2014
  598.7'2--dc23
                                      2014040096

Printed in the United States of America in Brainerd, Minnesota
1 2 3 4 5 6 7 8 9 0 18 17 16 15 14

122014
WEP051214

Project Coordinator: Heather Kissock   Designer: Mandy Christiansen

Weigl acknowledges Getty Images, Alamy, and iStock as the primary image suppliers for this title.

Animals in My Backyard

WOODPECKERS

CONTENTS

- 2   AV² Book Code
- 4   Meet the Woodpecker
- 6   Family
- 8   Strong Beak
- 10 Long Tongue
- 12 What He Eats
- 14 How He Flies
- 16 How He Talks
- 18 Where He Lives
- 20 Safety
- 22 Woodpecker Facts
- 24 Key Words

Meet the woodpecker.

He is a bird that people often hear knocking on trees.

He lives in a nest with his family when he is young.

When he is young, his mother and father both take care of him.

He has a strong beak.

A strong beak helps him peck holes in trees.

He has a very long tongue.

A very long tongue can reach food in small holes.

He feeds on insects found in trees.

In trees he also finds acorns and nuts to eat.

He flies like a butterfly.

Like a butterfly he flies along a wavy path.

He talks by drumming on trees.

Drumming on trees lets other woodpeckers know where he is.

He can be found in most parts of the world.

In most parts of the world he lives in forests.

If you meet the woodpecker, he may be afraid. He might fly away.

If you meet the woodpecker, stay back.

21

WOODPECKER FACTS

These pages provide more detail about the interesting facts found in the book. They are intended to be used by adults as a learning support to help young readers round out their knowledge of each animal featured in the *Animals in My Backyard* series.

Pages 4–5

Woodpeckers are birds that are best known for knocking on trees. There are about 180 species of woodpeckers. Depending on the species, woodpeckers may range in size from 3 inches (7.5 centimeters) to 24 inches (60 cm) long. The pileated woodpecker is the largest woodpecker commonly found in North America. It can be up to 19 inches (48 cm) long.

Pages 6–7

Woodpeckers live in a nest with their family when they are young. Parents work together to create a hole in a tree to serve as a nest. The female then lays between one and six eggs. Both parents help incubate the eggs, which takes between 11 and 18 days. The young are ready to leave the nest by about one month of age.

Pages 8–9

Woodpeckers have strong beaks. The woodpecker's beak is long and pointed. It uses its beak like a chisel to cut through tree bark and wood. A woodpecker can peck up to 20 times a second, or as many as 12,000 pecks in a day. Its thick skull has air pockets that cushion the woodpecker's brain. This protects it from the trauma associated with pecking. Special feathers keep wood chips from entering the nostrils.

Pages 10–11

Woodpeckers have very long tongues. A woodpecker's tongue can be up to 4 inches (10 cm) long. The tongue has a sticky substance on the end to help it latch on to food. Some species, such as the pileated woodpecker, have backward-facing barbs on the tongue that help pull food into the mouth. When not in use, the tongue curls up in the back of the woodpecker's head, between the skull and skin.

Pages 12–13  **Woodpeckers eat both plants and animals.** They are omnivores, although their primary food source is insects. They drill into trees in search of ants and other insects. Woodpeckers will also eat nuts, acorns, seeds, and fruit. They will even drill small holes in trees so they can eat the sap inside.

Pages 14–15  **Woodpeckers have a butterfly-like flight pattern.** Most fly in a slow, undulating fashion. Woodpeckers also fly in a repeating pattern. They beat their wings three or four times and then glide. The three or four beats are quick, and the woodpecker then glides with its wings held close to the body instead of spread out like most birds.

Pages 16–17  **Woodpeckers communicate by drumming on trees.** Unlike songbirds, woodpeckers are not capable of intricate vocalizations. They can make basic sounds, but most communicate by drumming. A woodpecker drums by hammering its beak onto a surface to produce sound. This can be done to defend territory, attract a mate, or communicate with a partner.

Pages 18–19  **Woodpeckers are found in most parts of the world.** They live on every continent except Australia and Antarctica. There are about 22 species of woodpeckers in North America. Most woodpeckers stay in one general area, although a few species migrate to warmer climates in the winter. Woodpeckers are found in deciduous, coniferous, and mixed forests. Some also live in deserts, where they find food in cacti.

Pages 20–21  **Woodpeckers are often found close to places where people live.** Some people go out looking for woodpeckers as part of a birdwatching activity. Others find woodpeckers pecking on trees in their backyards, if not on their houses. Woodpeckers are not dangerous and will fly away when people come too close.

KEY WORDS

Research has shown that as much as 65 percent of all written material published in English is made up of 300 words. These 300 words cannot be taught using pictures or learned by sounding them out. They must be recognized by sight. This book contains 53 common sight words to help young readers improve their reading fluency and comprehension. This book also teaches young readers several important content words. These words are paired with pictures to aid in learning and improve understanding.

Page	Sight Words First Appearance
4	the
5	a, he, hear, is, often, on, people, that, trees
6	and, both, family, father, him, his, in, lives, mother, of, take, when, with, young
8	has
9	helps
10	long, very
11	can, food, small
12	found
13	also, eat, finds, to
14	like
15	along
16	by, know, other, talks, where
18	be, most, parts, world
20	away, back, if, may, might, you

Page	Content Words First Appearance
4	woodpecker
5	bird
6	nest
8	beak
9	holes
10	tongue
12	insects
13	acorns, nuts
14	butterfly
15	path
19	forests

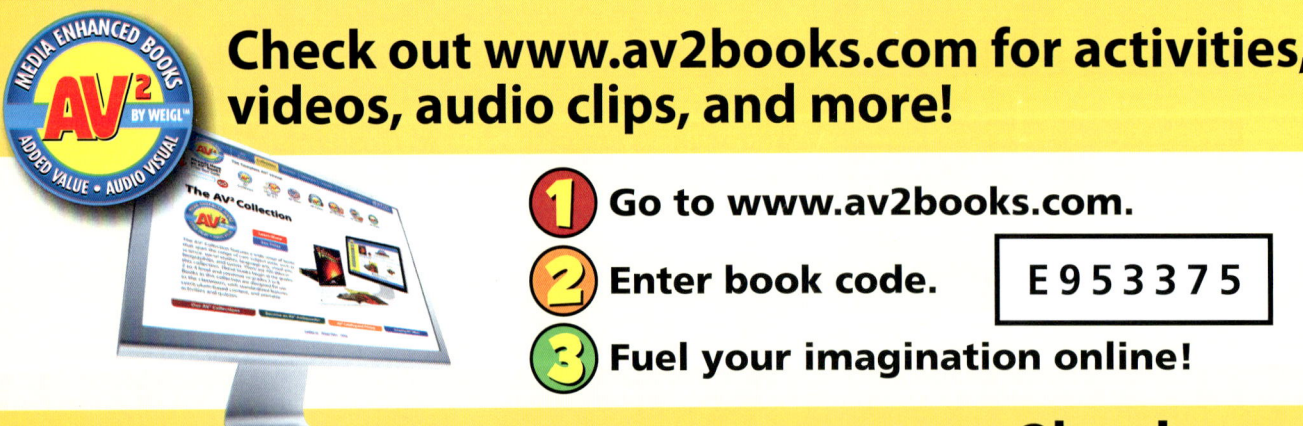

Check out www.av2books.com for activities, videos, audio clips, and more!

① Go to www.av2books.com.

② Enter book code.   E 9 5 3 3 7 5

③ Fuel your imagination online!

www.av2books.com